Ladybird I'm Ready... for Science!

Written by Steve Parker

Illustrated by Barbara Bongini

About this book

I'm Ready for Science is for children who want to learn about the world around them. It has been especially written to help children learning science in Years 1 and 2 at primary school.

It is clearly divided into four main subjects: plants, weather and seasons, animals and people, and materials. Ideal for homework and projects, it includes lots of ideas that will encourage children to investigate, try experiments and ask questions.

Consultant: Dr Deidre Holes, The Hamilton Trust

LADYBIRD BOOKS

UK | USA | Canada | Ireland | Australia
India | New Zealand | South Africa

Ladybird Books is part of the Penguin Random House group of companies
whose addresses can be found at global.penguinrandomhouse.com.

ladybird.com

Penguin
Random House
UK

First published 2016
001

Printed in China

A CIP catalogue record for this book is available from the British Library

ISBN: 978-0-241-23835-6

Science and scientists

Science is the study of the world around us. It finds answers to questions such as: What is this made of? How does that work? Where did this come from? Science is exciting – and it's fun, too.

Some scientists work in special places called laboratories, or labs. They carry out tests and record the results.

But there are lots of other kinds of scientists . . .

Botanists study plants. They discover new flowers in places from deserts to jungles.

Food scientists find out about growing and making the food we eat.

Contents

Introduction

Meteorologists watch the clouds, sun, wind and rain to forecast the weather.

Animal scientists learn about all kinds of creatures: big and small, harmless or fierce.

Medical scientists look at the body to learn what it does and how to treat illnesses.

Material scientists study materials like metals and plastics, and machines made from them.

Plants
Green world

There are many different types of plants, but they all need three things to grow – sunlight, nutrients from the soil and water from rain.

oak

monkey puzzle

daisies

bluebells

Trees are usually tall with one main woody stem, called the trunk.

Wild flowers are found in fields, hedges, woods and other natural places.

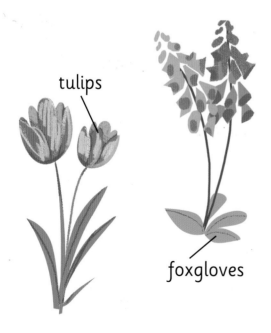

tulips

foxgloves

rose

laurel

Flowers in gardens and parks are planted by people. They are usually bright and colourful.

Bushes grow low to the ground with lots of woody stems. Some are very thorny!

Some trees keep their leaves all through the year. They are called evergreen trees.

maple

beech

ash

Some trees lose their leaves once a year – in autumn. They are called deciduous trees.

INVESTIGATE . . .

Find some leaves from an evergreen tree and some from a deciduous tree.

What do they look like?
How do they feel?

Plant parts

Plants like magnolia trees and tulips may look very different to each other, but they have the same main parts. Each part does a special job to help keep the whole plant alive.

Magnolia tree

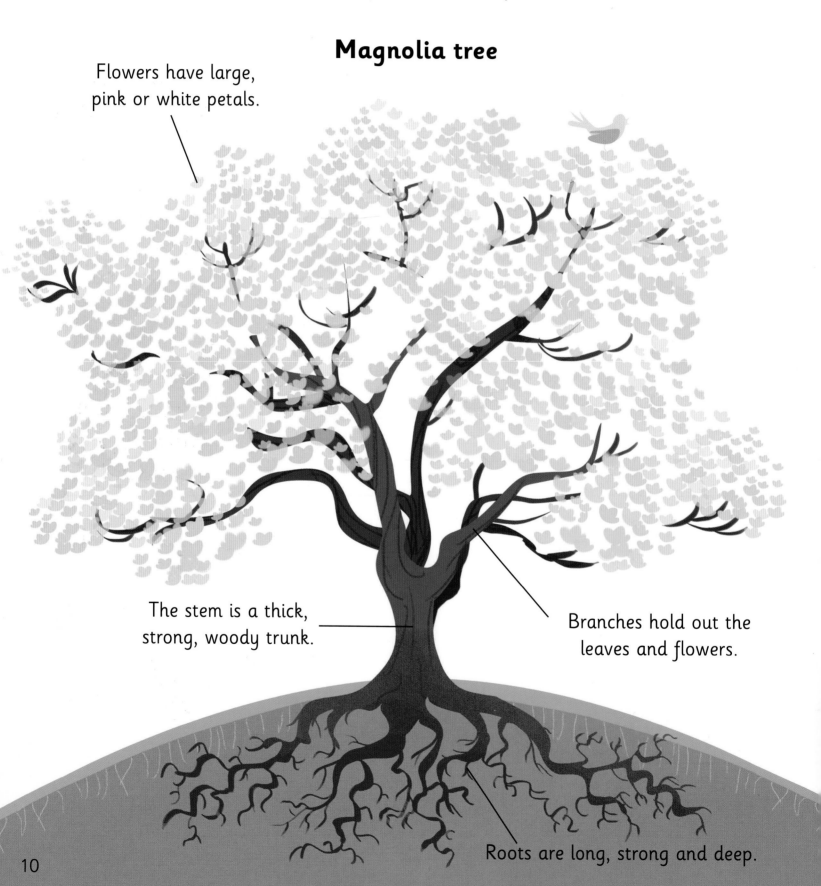

Flowers have large, pink or white petals.

The stem is a thick, strong, woody trunk.

Branches hold out the leaves and flowers.

Roots are long, strong and deep.

Tulip

The flower has a few small, red petals.

The stem holds up the flower.

bulb

Thin roots grow down into the soil.

What do plant parts do?

Flowers: make seeds which grow into new plants.

Leaves: take in light and make food for the plant.

Stems: hold up the leaves and flowers.

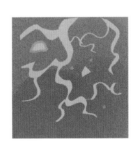
Roots: fix the plant in the soil, and take in water and nutrients.

COLLECT . . .

Collect leaves from plants that are different shapes and sizes. Put them in your science scrapbook, draw around them, and label the drawings with the plant names and time of year you found them.

Plants to eat

Fruits and vegetables come from plants. Some are eaten fresh or raw, while others need cooking first. They are very healthy to eat.

Fruits grow from a plant's flowers. Fruits contain seeds (called pips), stones or nuts.

Some examples of tree fruits are apples, pears and lemons.

Berries are small, soft fruits such as raspberries, strawberries and grapes. They grow on small plants or vines.

Tomatoes are often red but some are yellow or purple. They all come from the same type of plant.

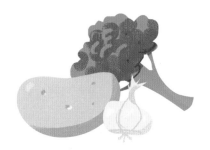

A vegetable may be the plant's leaves, or its stems, roots or bulbs.

Vegetable leaves are mostly green and juicy, like lettuce, cabbage and spinach.

Stems are usually long and slim, such as celery, spring onion and leek.

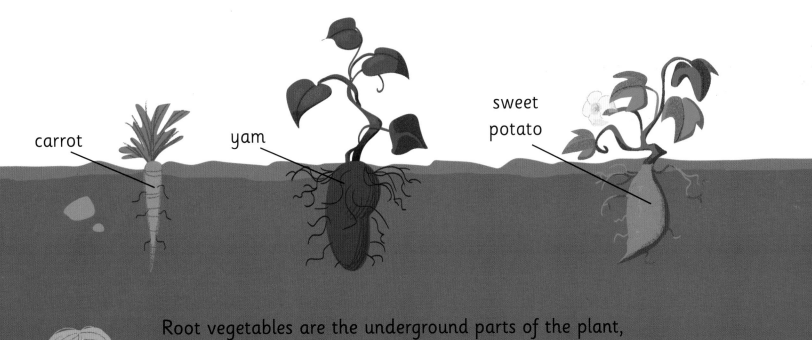

carrot

yam

sweet potato

Root vegetables are the underground parts of the plant, like carrots, yams and sweet potatoes.

INVESTIGATE . . .

Some of our foods are not named after their plants.

Can you find out which plants give us these foods?

- Crisps and chips
- Noodles and pasta
- Bread

Growing from seeds

Most plants begin as small seeds. They need soil, water, warmth and light to start growing.

How an oak tree grows
Each spring the tree makes small yellow-green flowers. These develop into acorns that fall from the tree in autumn.

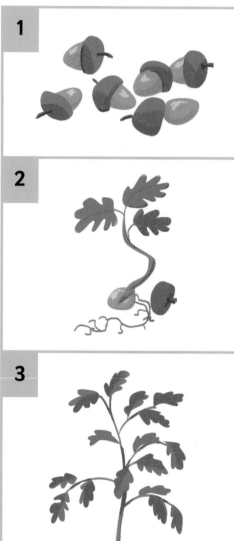

An oak-tree seed is called an acorn. It grows roots downward and a shoot grows upward. Then it develops leaves and gets taller each year.

Each year the oak tree grows taller and wider.
Its trunk has rings inside, one for each year. Some oaks are more than 500 years old!

How sunflowers grow

Sunflower seeds are made in the head of the flower.

In just a few weeks they grow into plants with beautiful yellow petals!

The seeds fall out of the flower when it dies.

INVESTIGATE . . .

- Grow your own seeds, such as beans or sunflowers.

- Follow the instructions on the packet.

- Keep some seeds in a cool, dark place, others in a warm, light place. Which grow best?

- Draw the results in your science scrapbook.

Weather and seasons
What is the weather?

The weather is all around us, all of the time. It can change from hot to cold, wet to dry, or calm to windy, or it can stay the same for days.

The Sun gives out light and heat. The heat warms the ground and then the air. This makes the air move.

Clouds are made of millions of tiny floating drops of water. In fine weather, clouds are white and fluffy. Low, dark clouds usually mean rain.

Wind is made by warm and cold air moving about. It blows the clouds along in the sky and brings changes in the weather.

Rain happens when tiny drops of water in a cloud join to make large drops that are too heavy to float. Then the drops fall from the sky.

Storms have fast winds and lots of rain. Thunderstorms have flashes of lightning, and loud cracks and booms of thunder.

DID YOU KNOW?

The fastest winds blow at over 400 kilometres per hour. This is four times faster than a car on a motorway!

Changing seasons

The weather changes gradually through the year.
These changes are called the seasons.

WINTER

Winter days are usually cold and cloudy, and there is often rain.
In very cold weather, the raindrops freeze and fall as snow.

SPRING

In spring, the days become warmer, with more daylight hours. There are fewer clouds
and less rain. Plants start to grow and flowers come out.

SUMMER

Summer days are warm or hot, with more bright sunshine. There is little wind and there might be no rain for weeks.

AUTUMN

Autumn days are cooler, with more rain and fewer daylight hours. There may be storms and the leaves fall from the trees.

INVESTIGATE . . .

In which season would you:

- Have a picnic at the seaside?
- Run through fallen leaves?
- Make a snowman?
- Visit a flower show?

Measure the weather

Weather forecasts show the likely weather over the next few hours or days. Making a record of the weather can help us work out what the weather will be like at a certain time.

Make a rain gauge

Fix a plastic funnel into a plastic drinks bottle using modelling clay.

Put the gauge where it can collect falling rain.

Each day, measure how much rain is in the bottle.

Draw a chart showing the rainfall each day. Which is wetter, summer or winter?

Measuring wind

Direction is where the wind blows from. For example, a west wind comes from the west – we also call it a westerly wind.

Strength is how fast the wind blows. Very strong winds are called gales and bring storms and damage.

INVESTIGATE . . .

Look up sunrise and sunset times where you live to find out how long the sun is in the sky for – that is, the hours of daylight. How does this differ from summer to winter?

Animals and people
All kinds of animals

There are millions of different kinds of animals in the world. They can be divided into groups by their body parts and whether they have warm or cold blood.

beetle   **ladybird**   **bee**

Insects have six legs and hard outer bodies. They are cold-blooded. Beetles, ladybirds and bees are all insects.

spider   **scorpion**

Arachnids look a bit like insects but they have eight legs and sharp fangs. They are cold-blooded. Spiders and scorpions are arachnids.

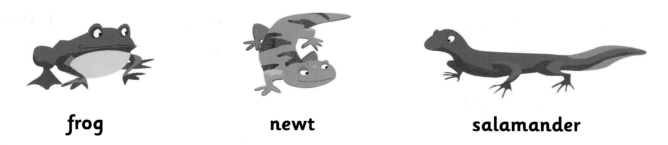

frog   **newt**   **salamander**

Amphibians are cold-blooded. They have damp, soft skin and live both in and out of water. Frogs, newts and salamanders are amphibians.

snake **chameleon** **tortoise**

Reptiles are cold-blooded with scaly skin. Snakes, chameleons and tortoises are all types of reptiles.

robin **penguin** **ostrich**

Birds are warm-blooded with feathers and beaks. They all have wings but not all can fly. Robins, penguins and ostriches are birds.

cow

whale

dog **lion** **dolphin**

Mammals are warm-blooded. Most of them, like dogs, cows and lions have hairy bodies and four legs, but whales and dolphins are mammals, too.

COLLECT . . .

Look out for signs of animals in your garden or neighbourhood and draw them in your science scrapbook:

bird feathers

nibbled leaves

snail shells

mammal fur

paw prints

Where animals live

Each kind of animal is suited to living in a certain place, called its habitat. The habitat provides all of the animal's needs, such as food, warmth, a nest or den, and shelter.

Microhabitats

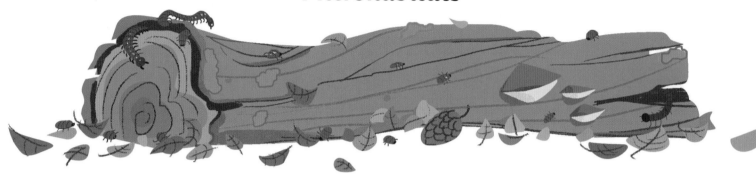

Underneath this old log is a very small habitat, called a microhabitat. The animals here like this dark, cool, damp place.

Woodlice, slugs and millipedes eat old wood and leaves. The centipede has a flat body to help it crawl into cracks.

Woodland

The woodland is a habitat with lots of trees and smaller plants that are food, shelter and homes for many creatures.

Badgers live in tunnels called setts. The squirrel makes its nest in a tree.

Deserts

The elf owl makes a nest hole in a cactus.

The hopping mouse has large feet to help jump on soft sand.

Deserts are very dry, with few trees and other plants. Animals often come out at night when it is much cooler.

INVESTIGATE . . .

Can you find out where these animals live?

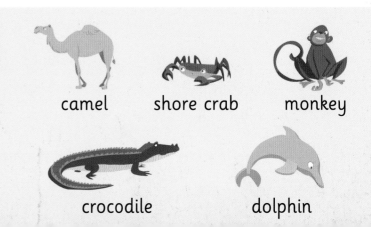

camel   shore crab   monkey

crocodile   dolphin

What animals eat

Animals can be put into three main groups, depending on the type of food they eat:

Animals that eat mainly plants are **herbivores**.

Animals that eat mainly other creatures are **carnivores**.

Animals that eat both plants and creatures are **omnivores**.

Different habitats contain very different plants, herbivores and carnivores. Yet in each habitat the living things link together to form a food chain.

Swamp

carnivore:
alligator

herbivore:
turtle

plants:
waterweeds

African grassland

carnivore:
lion

herbivore:
antelope

plants:
grasses

Mountains

carnivore:
mountain lion

herbivore:
mountain goats

plants:
shrubs and bushes

City

Town and city foods include our leftovers and rubbish.
They are eaten by omnivores such as raccoons, foxes and rats.

INVESTIGATE . . .

In your science scrapbook, make a list of pets and what they eat. Are they herbivores, carnivores or omnivores?

cat

tarantula

rabbit

dog

goldfish

parrot

Animals on the go

All animals move around and eat! But they do so in many different ways, using various parts of their bodies.

Moving around

A clownfish swims with its side fins and by waving its tail.

A snake slides along by wriggling its body from side to side.

A duck flies by flapping its two wings up and down.

A kangaroo leaps using its two strong back legs.

Feeding

A shark bites off lumps of food with its sharp teeth.

A frog flicks out its long, sticky tongue to catch flies.

A zebra nibbles grass with its front teeth and chews with its back teeth.

A vampire bat laps up blood.

DID YOU KNOW?

The great white shark has a huge mouth filled with rows of about 3,000 jagged-edged, sharp teeth.

Snakes cannot chew. Instead, they open their mouths very wide and swallow their prey whole!

29

Which parts are which?

People are like animals, with mostly the same body parts.
See how we compare to other creatures:

human

Only the head has fur, called hair.

Hands have fingers and a thumb for holding.

There is fur almost all over.

dog

There is no tail!

Legs are long and strong for running.

All four legs are about the same length.

The feet have claws for scratching.

A tail shows moods, such as wagging when happy!

mouse

The ears are almost as big as the head.

The long tail has no fur.

Long whiskers feel the way even in darkness.

Feet have claws to dig for food.

horse

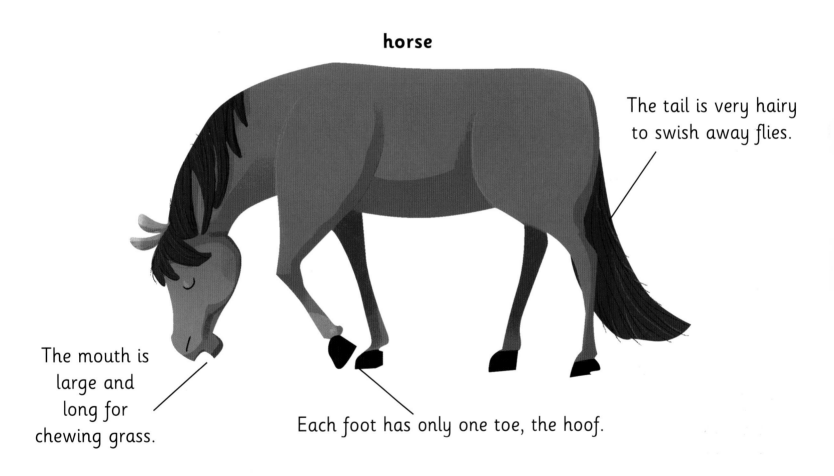

The tail is very hairy to swish away flies.

The mouth is large and long for chewing grass.

Each foot has only one toe, the hoof.

INVESTIGATE . . .

Can you find the same body parts on these mammals?

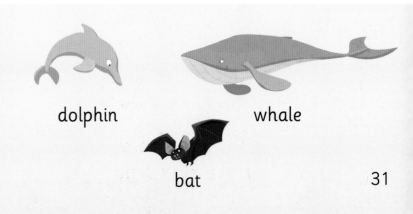

dolphin

whale

bat

Take care of yourself

The human body – your body – is very special. It feels better and more healthy if you take care of it all through the day.

A wash, shower or bath gets rid of dirt, pests and smells.

Breakfast is an important meal, giving energy for the morning ahead.

Learning is good for your brain. Riding a bike, school lessons and even playing with your friends are all types of learning.

Exercise, like playing sports and games, keeps muscles, joints and bones strong.

Having fun, like playing music, drawing or reading a book, helps to keep the body happy and healthy.

Brushing teeth after meals and before bedtime makes sure the teeth last a long time.

Everybody needs a good night's sleep. Going to bed too late, too often, causes headaches and other problems.

INVESTIGATE . . .

How much sleep does a person need? Ask your family and friends and make a list in your science scrapbook. Who needs more – children or grown-ups?

Feast for the senses

Animals, including humans, find out about the world using their senses. These are especially important at mealtimes.

The nose smells foods even before they are seen. This helps us to know what is in the meal.

The skin of the lips and mouth feel the food, and whether it is hot or cold, hard or soft.

The eyes see what the meal contains. Each food has its own colours and shapes.

The tongue tastes the flavours of the meal, such as sweet, sour, salty, bitter and savoury.

The ears hear the sounds of cooking, such as splashes, bubbles, hisses and sizzles.

DID YOU KNOW?

The body needs varied kinds of foods, but not too much of some.

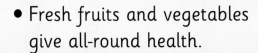 • Fresh fruits and vegetables give all-round health.

 • Bread, pasta, potatoes and rice have energy.

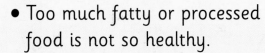 • Too much fatty or processed food is not so healthy.

Growing up

All living things grow from small to big. They also breed or reproduce – make more of their own kind. This is called the life cycle.

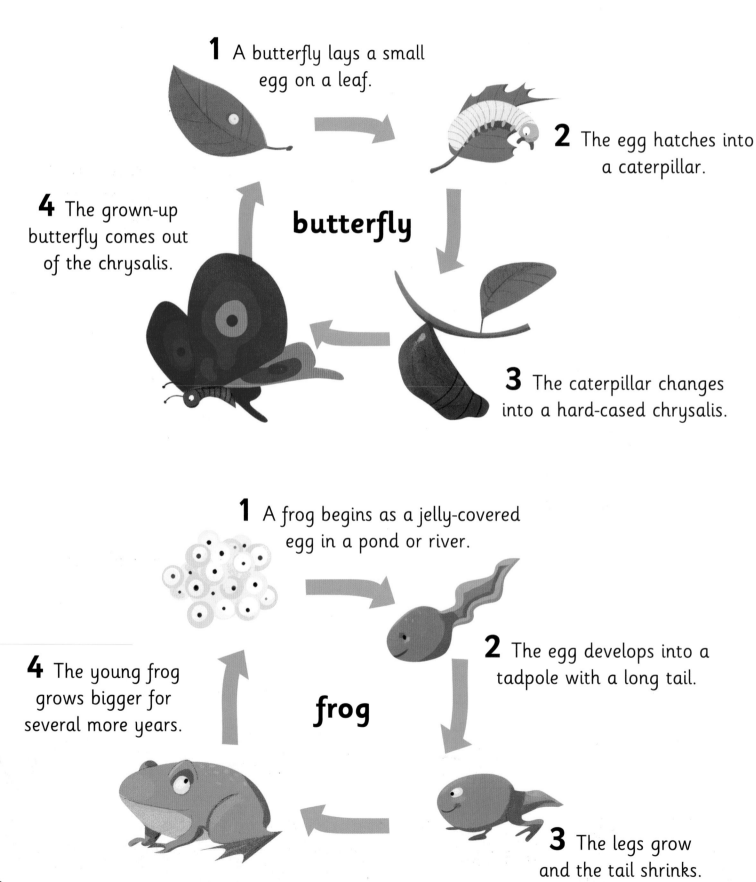

1 A butterfly lays a small egg on a leaf.

2 The egg hatches into a caterpillar.

butterfly

4 The grown-up butterfly comes out of the chrysalis.

3 The caterpillar changes into a hard-cased chrysalis.

1 A frog begins as a jelly-covered egg in a pond or river.

2 The egg develops into a tadpole with a long tail.

4 The young frog grows bigger for several more years.

frog

3 The legs grow and the tail shrinks.

1 A mother deer gives birth to her baby, called a fawn.

deer

2 The fawn can stand and run a short time after birth.

3 The mother deer feeds her fawn on her milk.

4 The fawn grows up and leaves its mother.

INVESTIGATE . . .

How do baby humans compare with other animals?
- Do they hatch from eggs?
- Do they run through fallen leaves?

Materials
Playground fun

A visit to the playground is great fun. It is also a place where you can investigate materials. Which materials are used, and why?

The bright paint looks good. It also protects the materials underneath.

The ground is covered with a strong foam. It is slightly bouncy in case of falls.

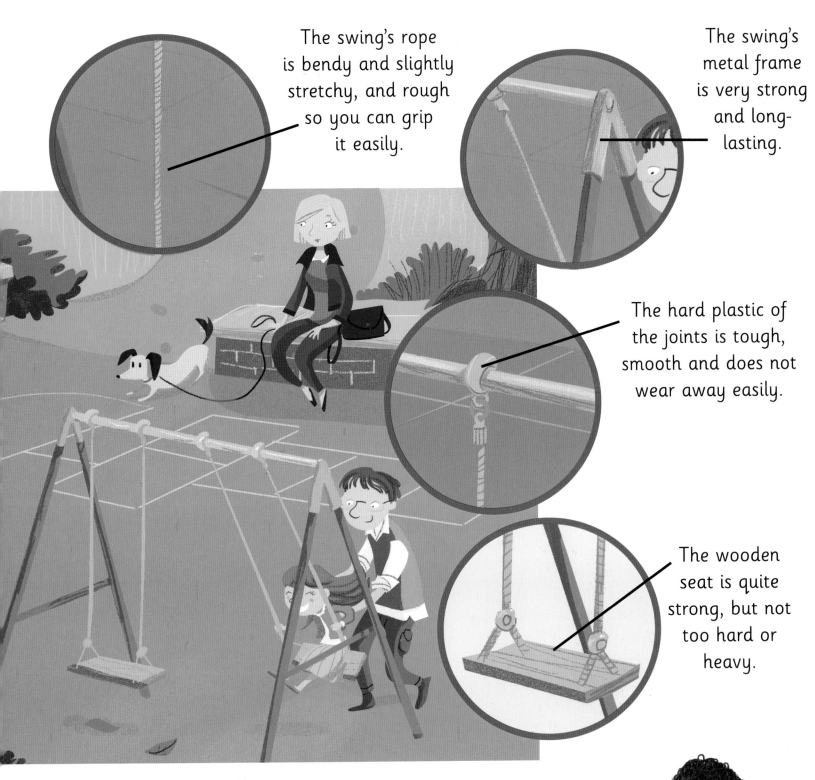

The swing's rope is bendy and slightly stretchy, and rough so you can grip it easily.

The swing's metal frame is very strong and long-lasting.

The hard plastic of the joints is tough, smooth and does not wear away easily.

The wooden seat is quite strong, but not too hard or heavy.

No materials last forever. So a person checks the playground often, to see what needs mending or replacing.

INVESTIGATE . . .

Make a list of materials at your local playground or play area in your science scrapbook.

Which material is most common?

Making materials

Some materials are natural, from the ground or as parts of plants and animals. Other materials are made by people and are called artificial or synthetic materials. Each has its own features or properties.

Wood **Source:** trees

Good properties: quite light, can be easily cut and shaped

Bad properties: if it gets damp, it can rot and break

Stone **Source:** rocks in the ground

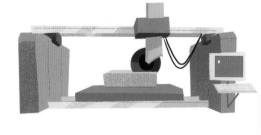

Good properties: hard, heavy, lasts for thousands of years

Bad properties: difficult to cut and shape

Glass

Source: made by heating sand and other substances

Good properties: hard, smooth, see-through, long-lasting

Bad properties: Breaks easily into sharp pieces

Plastic

Source: made from oil from the ground

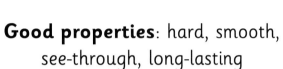

Good properties: can be made into almost any shape and colour, lasts a long time

Bad properties: goes rough and cracked, and does not rot away naturally

INVESTIGATE . . .

Gather plastic items like a plastic bag, plastic drinks bottle, plastic cup and plastic toys.

Are all plastics the same?

41

Using materials

Many items can change because of the materials they are made from. They may be bent, stretched, soaked or melted.

House bricks are hard, strong, rough and long-lasting. Their material may look like natural stone but is really made in a factory.

An elastic band is made from a solid material. Yet it pulls and stretches easily, then springs back to its original size.

Cooking foil is made from a metal called aluminium. It is shiny and smooth. It is also so thin, it can easily bend and fold.

A sponge feels very light and soft. But when it soaks up water into its holes, it becomes many times heavier.

Chocolate is normally solid. But warm it with your fingers and it melts into a runny, sticky liquid. Yum!

INVESTIGATE . . .

How do these objects and materials compare with each other?

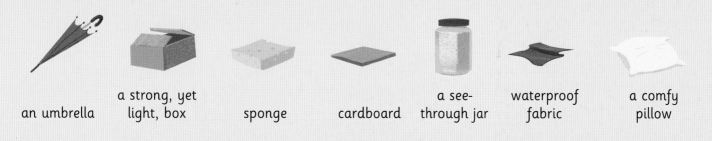

an umbrella   a strong, yet light, box   sponge   cardboard   a see-through jar   waterproof fabric   a comfy pillow

Which material is best?

Similar items can be made from different materials, for different uses. Some materials are also so useful, they make hundreds of different items.

Not all rubber is the same. Some kinds are harder and stiffer than others.

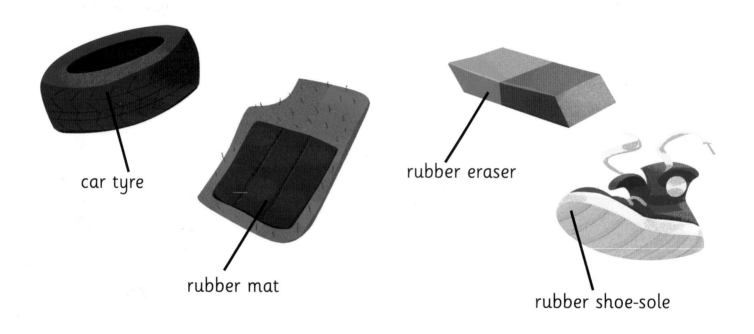

car tyre

rubber mat

rubber eraser

rubber shoe-sole

This pottery fruit bowl looks good, with colours and patterns.

This metal food-mixer bowl is strong and does not crack.

This plastic food bowl is lightweight and easy to wipe clean.

Find out which scientists invented which of these materials:

Leo Baekeland

Charles Goodyear

Joseph Aspdin

hardened rubber

plastics

cement

COLLECT . . .

Some materials can be collected to use again (this is called recycling). It saves money, energy and natural resources. What do you recycle in your home or school? Could you recycle more?

plastics bin

metals bin

paper bin

Glossary

artificial

something that has been made by people, rather than being made naturally

carnivore

an animal that eats other animals

deciduous

a tree or shrub that loses its leaves every year, usually in the autumn

evergreen

a tree or shrub that has green leaves throughout the year

habitat

the natural home of an animal or plant

herbivore

an animal that only eats plants

investigate

to look at, or study, a subject or a problem

materials

the substance, or group of substances that something is made from

nutrient

a substance that provides the useful things for life and growth

omnivore

an animal that eats both plants and animals

recycle

to turn waste or rubbish into reusable materials

reproduce

to breed, or make more of their own kind

Index